Visual World

العالم المصور

المساجد والجوامع
Mosques

50+ Engaging Colouring Activities
to Celebrate the Beauty of Islamic Places of Worship

Mosaic Tree Press

ISBN 978-1-916524-48-4

Copyright © 2023 Mosaic Tree Press

All rights reserved. No part of this book may be reproduced, stored in a retrieval system, or transmitted in any form or by any means, electronic, mechanical, photocopying, recording, or otherwise, without the prior written permission of the author.

All artwork was designed and licensed by Freepik.com

First printing, 2023

Published by Mosaic Tree Press
Browse our complete catalogue of publications at MosaicTree.org

In the name of God, the Most Gracious, the Most Merciful

Contents

Section 1 — The Kaʿbah & Masjid al-Haram (اَلْمَسْجِدُ ٱلْحَرَام) (i.e. The Sacred Mosque or The Great Mosque of Mecca)

Section 2 — Al Masjid an Nabawi (The Prophet's Mosque), Medina, Saudi of Arabia

Section 3 — Al-Aqsa Mosque (جامع الأقصى) & the Dome of the Rock (قبة الصخرة), Jerusalem, Palestine

Section 4 — The Blue Mosque (aka The Sultan Ahmed Mosque), Istanbul, Turkey

Section 5 — Mosques from Around the World

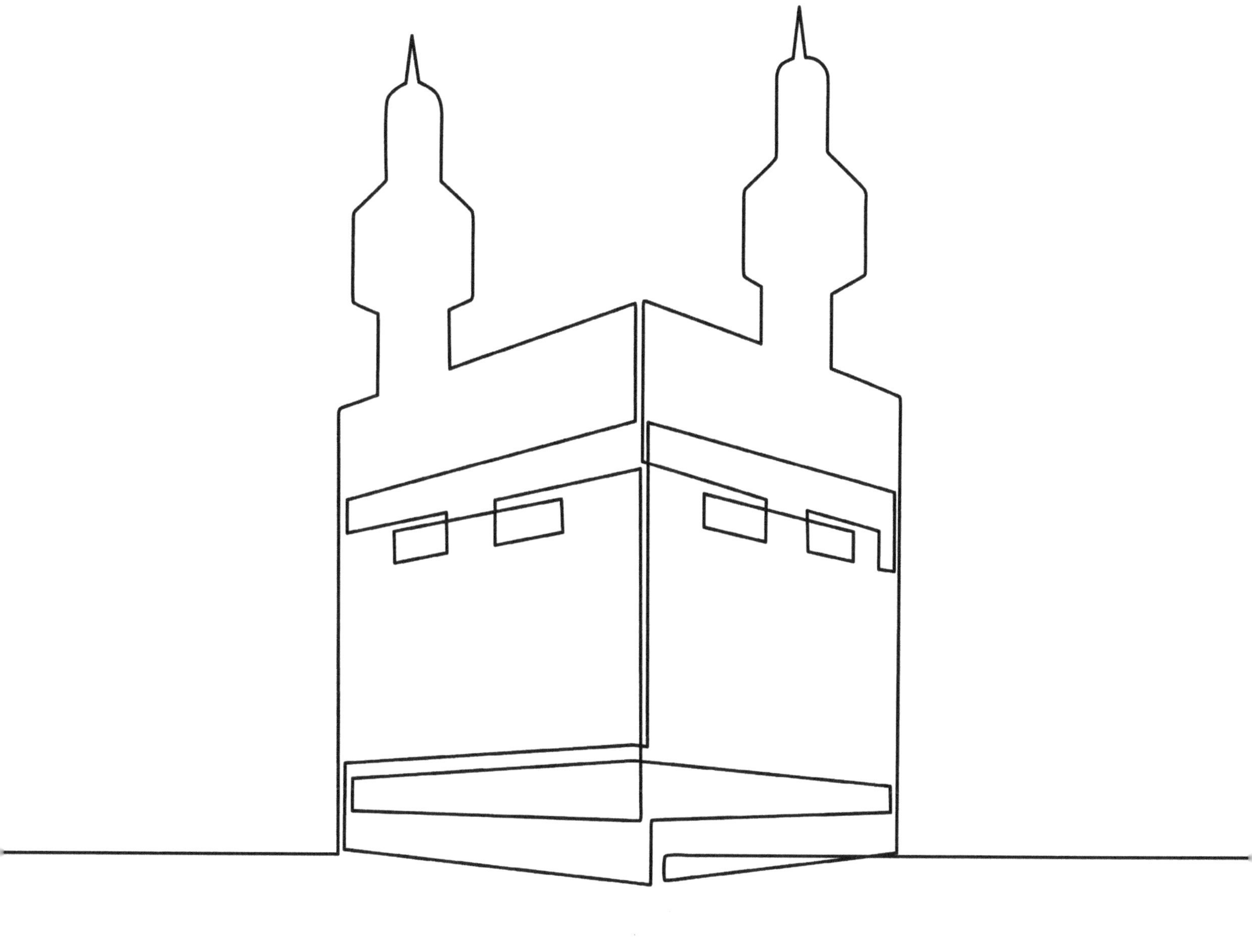

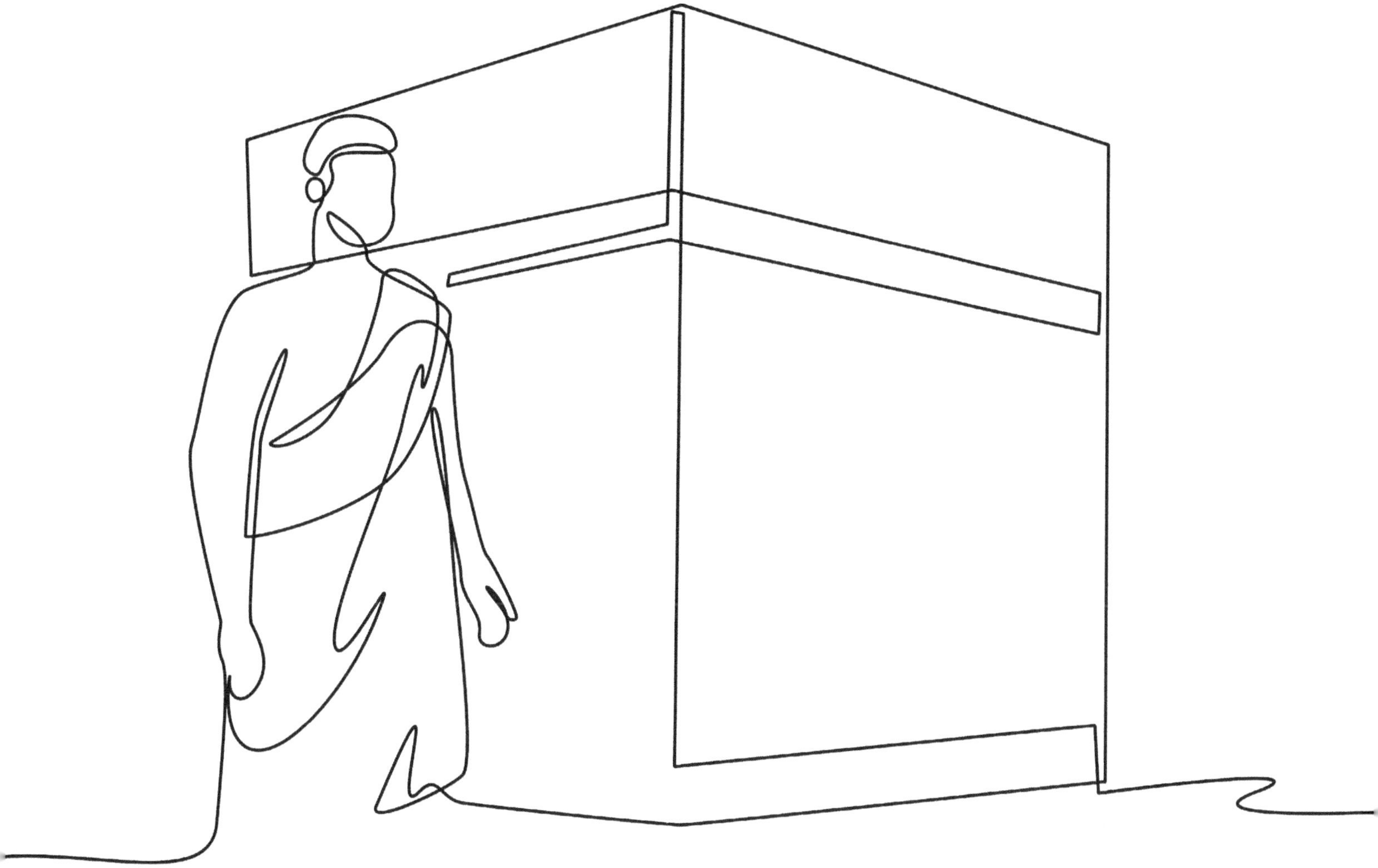

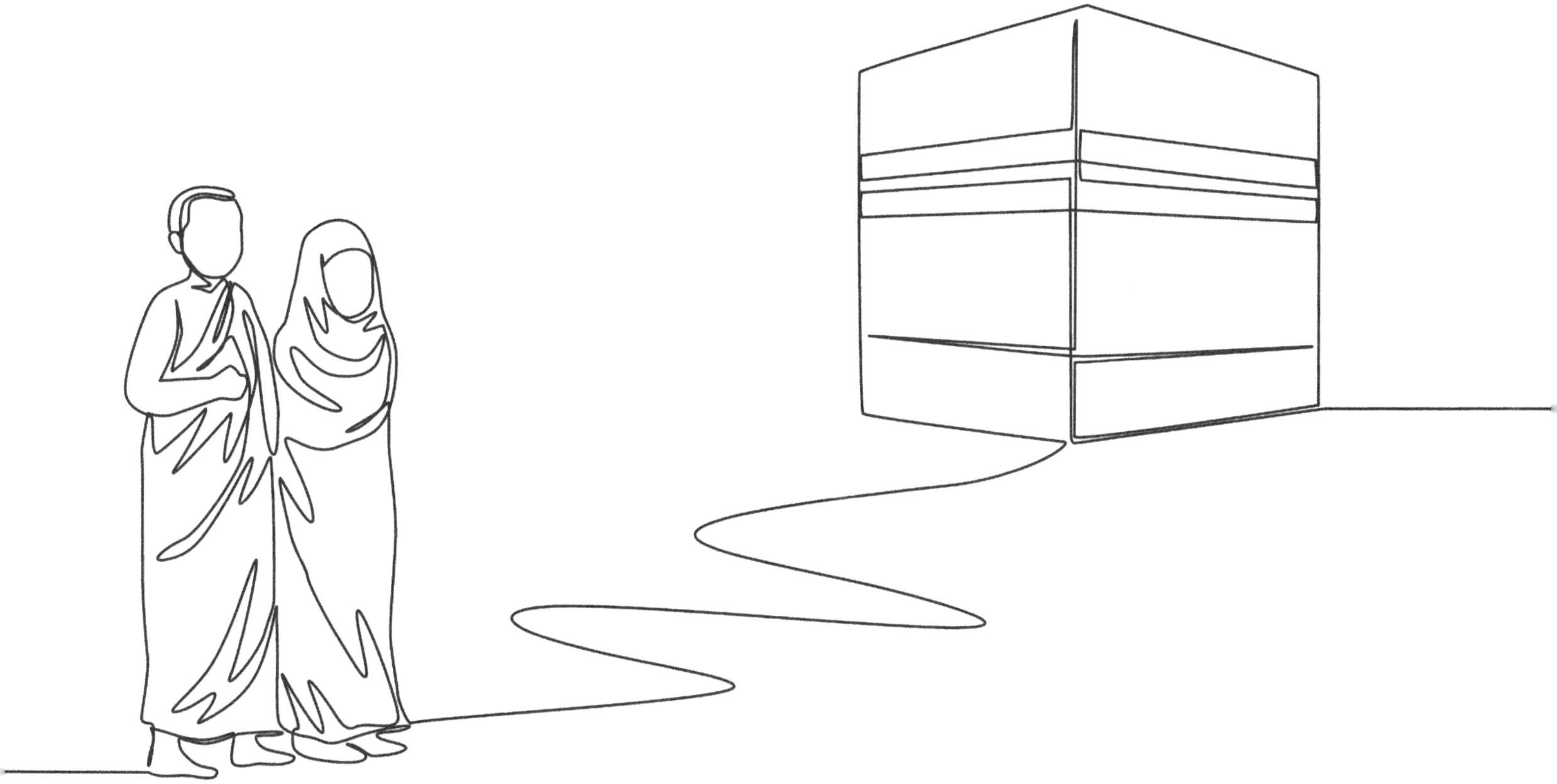

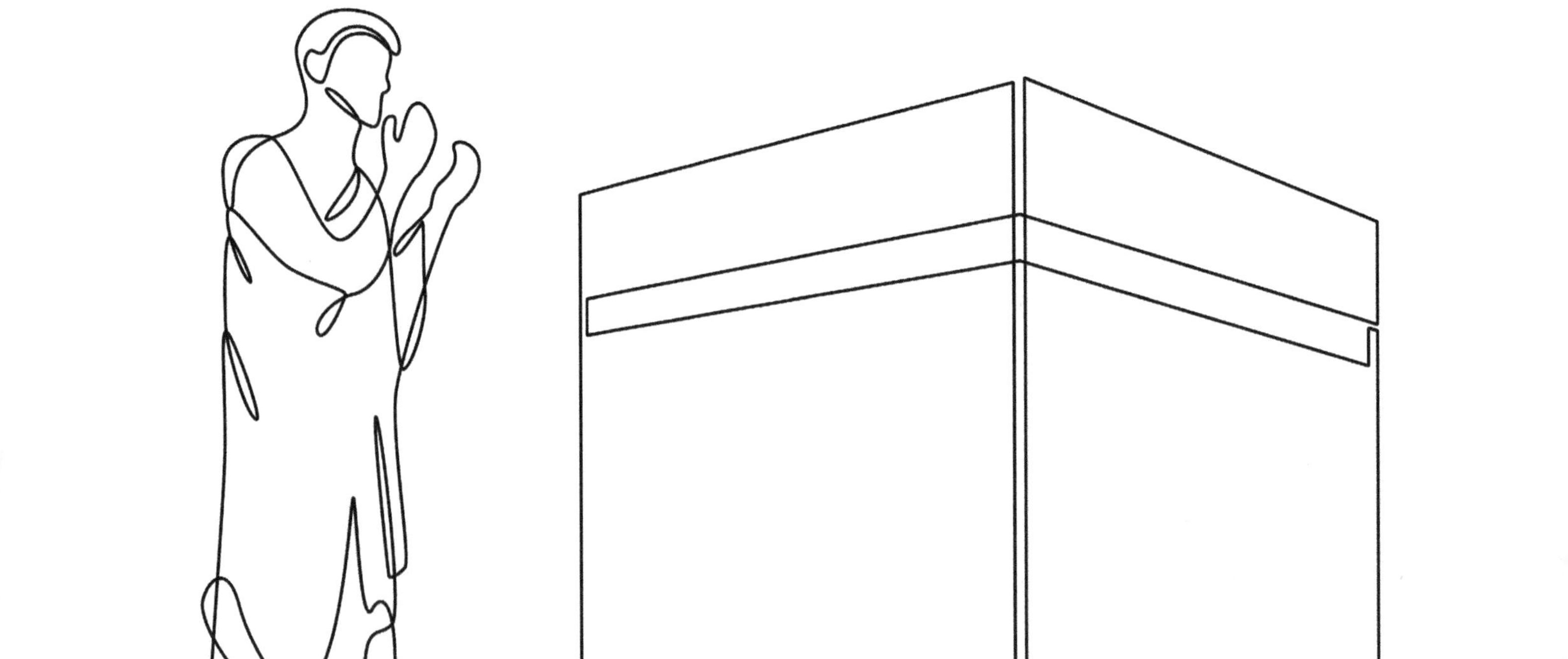

Dome of the Rock

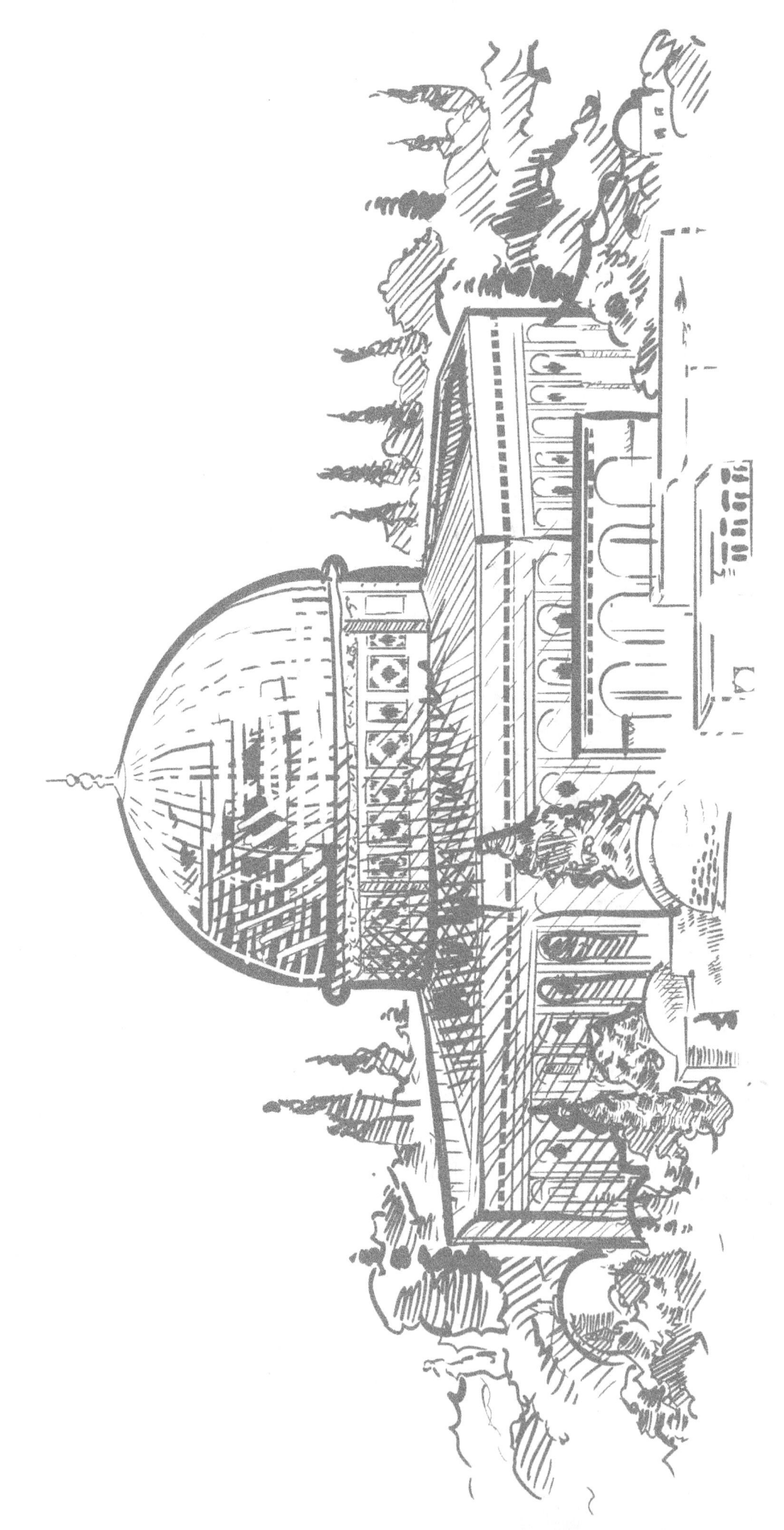

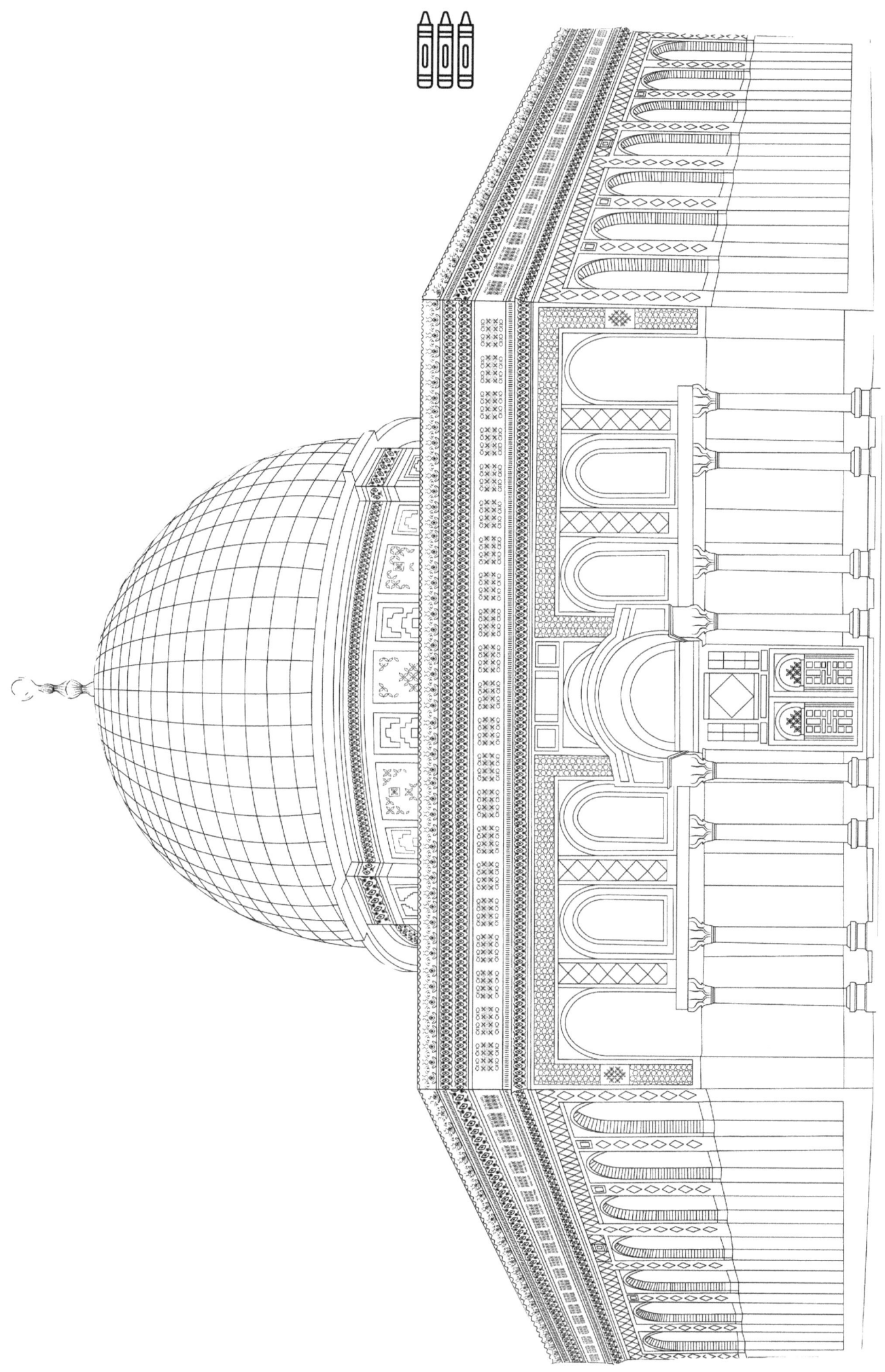

Publications by Mosaic Tree Press

An ABC of Quotes About Palestine: Exploring Voices on Palestine & the Palestinian Quest for Justice (2023)

An Abc of Palestine: A Journey To Discover Palestine & The Palestinian People For Kids & Grown Ups (2023)

Palestine: 200+ Cut-Out & Collage Images for Arts & Crafts Activities (2023)

Palestine: 50+ Colouring Activities to Celebrate Palestine & the Palestinian People (2023)

My Journey Through The Most Beautiful Names of Allah: Arabic Reader & Activity Book for Kids: **(Volume 1, 2 & 3)** (2023)

My First Arabic Alphabet & Colouring Book [Arabic for Little Ones] (2023)

My First Arabic Alphabet: Letter Tracing & Colouring Book [Arabic for Little Ones] (2023)

Essential Arabic Readers: Alphabet Letters with Vowels & Pronunciation Symbols, Mosaic Tree Press (2022)

Similar Sounding Letters in Arabic: Essential Arabic Readers (2023)

Essential Arabic Readers: Arabic Alphabet Writing Practice Handbook, Mosaic Tree Press (2023)

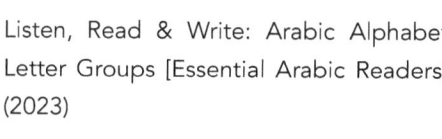
Listen, Read & Write: Arabic Alphabet Letter Groups [Essential Arabic Readers] (2023)

My First Arabic Numbers Reader & Colouring Book, Mosaic Tree Press (2023)

My First Arabic Colours: Reader & Activity Book for Kids, Mosaic Tree Press (2023)

My Arabic Animal Alphabet Reader, Arabic for Little Ones, Mosaic Tree Press (2023)

My First Arabic Alphabet Reader [Arabic for Little Ones] (2023)

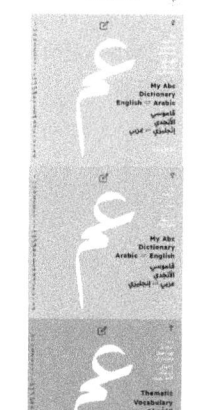
My Arabic Learning Journals: My Abc Dictionary (English-Arabic), Mosaic Tree Press (2022)

My Arabic Learning Journals: My Abc Dictionary (Arabic- English), Mosaic Tree Press (2022)

My Arabic Learning Journals: Thematic Vocabulary, Mosaic Tree Press (2022)

I Am .... An ABC of Empowering Self-Affirmations: A Guided Journal for Self-Discovery, Self-Growth & Resilience (2022)

My Journey through Ramadan & Eid Al-Fitr (Arabic for Little Ones), Mosaic Tree Press (2023)

CoronaVirus Lexicon: A Practical Guide for Arabic Learners & Translators (M. Diouri & M. Aboelezz 2023)

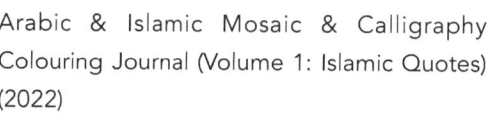
Arabic & Islamic Mosaic & Calligraphy Colouring Journal (Volume 1: Islamic Quotes) (2022)

Browse our full catalogue at
MosaicTree.org

 Arabic Script & Sounds   Arabic Vocabulary

 Arabic for Little Ones   Arabic/Islamic Mosaic & Calligraphy

 Arabic Learning Journals   Well-Being & Character Development

Completed with the grace of God

www.ingramcontent.com/pod-product-compliance
Lightning Source LLC
Chambersburg PA
CBHW080942040426

42444CB00015B/3414